CAFETERIA OF OVER

75

GAMES

CHILDREN PLAY IN

• Parties • Picnics • Birthdays • Schools • Parks
• Gatherings • Neighbourhood & at Home

CAFETERIA OF OVER

75 GAMES

CHILDREN PLAY IN

• Parties • Picnics • Birthdays • Schools • Parks
• Gatherings • Neighbourhood & at Home

Abhilasha Mathur

PUSTAK MAHAL®

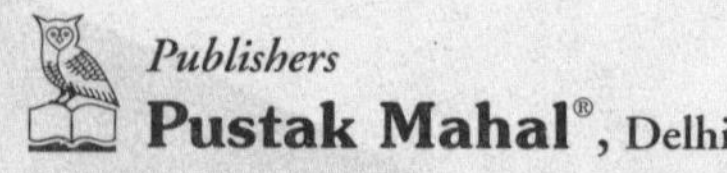

Administrative office and sale centre

J-3/16 , Daryaganj, New Delhi-110002
☏ 23276539, 23272783, 23272784 • *Fax:* 011-23260518
E-mail: info@pustakmahal.com • *Website:* www.pustakmahal.com

Branches

Bengaluru: ☎ 080-22234025 • *Telefax:* 080-22240209
E-mail: pustak@airtelmail.in • pustak@sancharnet.in
Mumbai: ☎ 022-22010941, 022-22053387
E-mail: rapidex@bom5.vsnl.net.in
Patna: ☎ 0612-3294193 • *Telefax:* 0612-2302719
E-mail: rapidexptn@rediffmail.com

ISBN 978-81-223-1259-1

Edition 2013

Printed at : Tarun Printers, Delhi

PREFACE

I wrote this book for children who are in need of recreational and playful environment between the monotonous academics. Education remains incomplete, if not supplemented with sufficient doses of games or other play-way methods. Children learn more quickly in a situation that they enjoy than in one that is full of tension. Their confidence is bound to increase with lots of playing experiences. Therefore, the little ones should be provided with choices of games focusing on visual, verbal, logical and analytical faculties for their overall personality development.

Most of these games have been used by me as a parent as well as an anchor of neighbourhood children's club. The games in this book are most suitable for playing during day-to-day gatherings of children in schools, neighbourhood, parks, birthdays and other parties. The children's games manual has been categorised into 3 parts for the ease of the users.

Part 1	Comprises of games involving a lot of movement of the body, physical jigsaws and running around.
Part 2	Aims at those moments when children are resting or sitting idle or even lying down, yet desire to play a game.
Part 3	Consists of a set of activities which kids can enjoy anytime and anywhere.

These games blow a spark inside the childs' mind setting him/ her to go and explore the world in and out.

My family has been a constant support in this journey of games.

●●

INTRODUCTION

Parents of the young ones are often in search of ways through which they can swing some magic in the air on their little ones to improve their concentration, alertness and liveliness.

This book is sure to help the lazy and directionless youngsters to become systematic and full of energy. With every game they face new challenges.

The illustrated games in every page of this book provide the techniques to channelise the child's energy towards a productive outcome for each activity they indulge into.

I present here a cafeteria of fun games and activities that will increase the attention span for children. This way they express and understand well and are pumped in with lots of pride and self-confidence. These games bring across lots of constructive, innovative and playful methods that help the children in improving their alertness, listening ability, memory, reasoning power, communication, creativity, observation, vocabulary and quite important among all, the reading and writing skills.

After spending great time with young minds I firmly believe that kids learn quickly when they enjoy. During my constant interaction with the children, I started the process of evolving new games that could facilitate their overall development. Combining games and playful methods with everyday education not only allows the child to express fully but also helps in understanding things better.

This book is a tool to bolster the parental support that can do wonders with the playing time of kids. Parents or other elders can give direction and pre-structure their play rather than letting them discover on their own. As facilitators in the games and activities, parents can also channelise the children's mind to think and act according to their age and track it in a more systematic manner.

While assisting children in their play, parents are often reminded of all the games they played years ago. I hope with the help of these games parents will get the children involved in more productive activities during the leisure hours to strike a balance between their physical and mental growth. As facilitator, parents and other elders have a very crucial role during the child's playing experience and growth. They would also enjoy being a part of these games.

●●

TIPS

FOR THE FACILITATOR

★ Collect and organise the children and make all arrangements prior to every game and always be present at the game site.

★ Select a clean surface as the playing area. Make sure that children enjoy every moment of the game and also follow all safety measures during the game.

★ The household items used in various games should be clean, light weight and have blunt edges. Sharp objects can be damaging to the children.

★ Always respect the child's imaginative ideas and suggestions during the preperation of the game or while playing. Don't ridicule their ideas or be sarcastic about them.

★ Break the ice in between the children and bring them in a playful mood. Always try to maintain a light and humorous atmosphere where the children feel jolly and comfortable. Long spells of silence during the game may lead to boredom. Playful comments during the game may make the children at ease.

★ Supervise and set some ground rules for the children playing the game. Restrict the time period given to players during the game. This makes the game more competitive.

★ Used rough paper with one side ruled can be provided during the game. This teaches children to save paper. Encourage the use of pencil for any writing work during the game so that papers can be re-used for other games.

★ Kindly be accurate while recording the various parameters such as time, distance, number of items, number of steps etc during the games. For all the card games, you may use thick white paper preferably ivory sheet, cut into uniform size and shape.

★ Games that require to prepare questions of general knowledge, photos and picture cards of animals, birds, flags, famous personalities, machines, logos of companies, fruits, places, monuments, etc may be of help.

★ For various games the time frame may be modified according to the age, size of the group and the availability of the actual playing time.

1 Play while running and moving

2 Play while sitting and Relaxing

3 PLAY ANYTIME AND ANYWHERE

Play while running and moving

This section of the book comprises of games with lots of physical exercises for the children. These games involve movement of the entire body while balancing, jumping, and running, crawling, racing or kicking. All the games encourage the children's independence, boost their self-confidence and help to break the monotony of their day to day routine. Apart from sweating out during the games, the young players have the opportunity for developing various types of learning skills. Open grounds, building corridors, school playgrounds and parks are suitable for games enlisted in this section.

Throwing Things at Your Back

This game would help players to improve their logical thinking skills as well as the response time the child takes for an action.

Before playing the facilitator needs to select a comfortable and clean playing area and draw a circle on the floor or mark a distinct portion on the ground.

The facilitator can choose any one player to begin the game. He/she has to be provided with a bag filled with 10 objects. He/she needs to throw the objects one by one at the back in the circle.

All the players take their turn to throw the same items.

The player who is able to throw all 10 objects in the circle in the minimum time wins the game.

Beware of the Sharks

Children need to know that a shark is a big fish living in the sea.

Chalks can be used to mark patches in the play area to designate islands.

The facilitator has to label a few players as sharks.

As the game starts the rest of the players run around to reach at any of the safe islands.

The killer sharks run around in the sea just to catch their prey.

The player can not stand in an island for more than 10 counts.

Each round of the game continues for one minute.

The lucky players manage to be safe from the jaws of the shark and win the game.

03 Rooms of the House

This game helps children to learn the names of various household items as well as the different types of activities that take place in the defined portions of the house.

Before the game starts, each player is assigned the names of various rooms/ partitions of the house. E.g., kitchen, drawing room, washroom, etc.

If there are many players, then more players can be assigned with a similar name.

To start the game the facilitator has to call out the names of household items like, the book, cup, waterjug, flowervase, wallclock, sofaset etc. or the names of various activities such as washing clothes, reading, dining, playing, etc.

As soon as the players hear the activity name or the item names they start jumping on their own position if they have any involvement in that action. E.g., if the called out word is waterjug or action word like drinking, then the players assigned the name kitchen, dining room need to jump at their position.

Players doing any wrong action would be out of the game.

Those jumping successfully till the end win the game.

04 The Number Plate Game

Apart from a lot of physical activity, this game promotes problem solving skills and gives practice for number identification. The ideal place to play this game is a neighbourhood parking lot.

According to the child's age various problems can be set, e.g. –

Find a 3-digit number.

Find a number which is odd.

Find an even number.

Find a number which is a multiple of 5.

Find a vehicle with a number from Delhi.

Find a vehicle with a number from Haryana.

Modern kids have an affinity towards vehicles, so they would jump at every problem and readily solve it.

A certain time limit can be set to give the kids a natural boast.

Encourage the winners with their deserved shares.

Traffic Lights

The game aims at teaching the children the rules of traffic light in addition to improving their motor skills and concentration power.

They need to know, red is to STOP, green is to GO and yellow is to GET READY.

The red, yellow and green paper sheets work like traffic lights.

The fun factor is multiplied if the game is played with a large group of children and in an open space.

A few children can be provided with red, yellow and green paper sheets. They can use the sheets in any innovative style so that they typically symbolise the traffic lights, e.g., circular cutouts, use of red, green or yellow household objects, vegetables or fruits.

When the game begins all the kids freely move in the playing area.

As soon as they face a red, green or yellow colour in front of them, they stop, keep moving or get ready respectively.

Players who do any wrong action would be out of the game.

Winners would be roaming till the end.

The Newspaper Bridge

The game is exciting. It promotes reading skills and improves ones concentration power.

Each player has to be provided with a set of newspapers arranged in a row, kept one after the other.

The players read marked set of news items from the newspapers kept for them and move ahead to read the next piece of paper arranged in the path.

The path has two end points, start and finish. The papers are arranged in between these points as if making a bridge.

The facilitator needs to mark the reading material of uniform length and quality before the game begins. He should also decide the reading content according to the age of the players.

Children finish their task and try to reach the finish point as fast as possible.

The facilitator has to check whether the reading is correct.

Player who succeeds in reading all the assigned contents in the minimum time wins.

HANG ON

Children love messing around with household items especially those that interest them more.

The game is to sharpen their logical skills and presence of mind.

Their toys, tiny stationeries and other small household items can be used.

Provide every player with a hanger.

Within a fixed duration the players are supposed to hang on maximum number of items on their hangers.

The use of safety pins, stapler and thread can further facilitate the players.

The little ones can be rewarded with some of their favourite item.

08 Follow Instructions

This game is a good warming up exercise.

When the players arrive in the play area, the facilitator starts the game by calling different instructions for them.

Number codes can also be set for each instruction so that when actually playing only the number is called.

Examples of some instructions are jump on heels, shake hands with one another, sit, rotate the head, hop back and fore, lay flat on the ground, stand, etc.

The facilitator can decide as to how many instructions are to be used according to the availability of time and the age of the player.

As the game proceeds the players who miss out on any instruction are considered out of that round.

After a number of rounds only one player is left who should be declared as the winner.

09 BODY IN ACTION

This game teaches the players to be alert and quick.

To start the game, the facilitator has to call out action words which the children are familiar with – eating, sitting, standing, running, writing, reading, seeing, jumping, etc.

On listening to each action, the player is supposed to say the name of the body part involved in that act.

Every player should be provided a time frame of half a minute for four different actions.

The facilitator can also set different time frames for the game according to the age of the players.

Players who speak the maximum correct names of body parts win the game.

10 Ask me at the Station

This game helps to improve the general knowledge.

Children enjoy holding each other from the waist and run around. This game gives them an opportunity to make a train in similar fashion.

As the children move their train in the playing area, the facilitator has to stand at a spot forming an imaginary station.

When the train halts at the station, the facilitator asks the first player a general knowledge question. After the player replies, he moves to the other end and the train proceeds.

When it halts next at an imaginary station, the facilitator asks another general knowledge question from the first player of the train. The game goes on as the train moves on.

11 Revolving like Planets Around the Sun

It is a game full of rotating movements.

One player can act like the sun and others as various planets. They revolve around it in concentric rings just like planets around the sun. The bigger planets rotate slowly.

Those nearer to the sun revolve faster in concentric rings.

Alongside, the players that act like planets also rotate in their own positions according to their size.

A chalk can be used to draw rings around the sun.

Kids enjoy the circular movement of their body. They feel elated when called by big names such as EARTH, JUPITER or VENUS.

12 Hop to the Shop

Before starting, the facilitator has to group some household items and arrange at different locations in the play area. These locations can then be designated as respective shops such as chemist, vegetable shop, grocery store, garment store, confectionary, dairy, bakery, jeweller, hardware store, etc.

When playing in the house, actual items can be used. When not at home, name slips of various items can be used.

To begin the game, sample items need to be scattered on the play area.

Children are then supposed to pick items from the ground and carry it to the right shop to buy that item. Those players who are unable to hop to the correct shop are considered out of the game.

Those who hop with the maximum correct items are the winners.

City Tags

This game improves alertness and acts as a good warming up exercise.

This game can be enjoyed more with a large group of players.

For this game the facilitator has to prepare a set of big paper tags each carrying a city's name on it.

The facilitator can make teams so that a part of the group wears the city tags and the other half does the running around.

When the game starts, the facilitator quickly calls out names of the labelled cities one after the other and the rest of the players run and touch that player.

After every 30 seconds the facilitator makes a pause to check the positions of the runners. Any player at the wrong destination is considered out. Again when the game starts the action of the teams can be interchanged.

As the game proceeds, players running successfully till the end win the game.

THE WAVES

This game can be played with a large group of children.

All the players need to form a big circle by holding each other's hands.

The game can start from any point in the circle.

Rule of the game is that the first three players sit and the next three stand, next three again sit and the next three again stand and so on.

This kind of action will lead to the formation of a wave.

As soon as any player does a wrong action, the wave gets disturbed and that particular player is considered out of the game.

The facilitator has to keep the game going at a fast pace so that with every round the number of players is cut down.

The wave continues for 5 minutes.

Players who are safe till the end win the game.

15 Seek out the Objects

This game helps players to develop problem solving skills.

The objects used for the game can be the household items like books, clothes, toys, etc.

The facilitator needs to hide the items at different locations.

The hunt can be made interesting by inserting certain clues for the children.

Clues such as–look near the window/open the book near the dictionary for the next clue/look for blue bag for more information.

This hunt would go on until the objects are found.

Make a Chain of Ribbons

This game can be enjoyed maximum in a large group that can be divided into teams by the facilitator.

The facilitator can provide a set of different coloured ribbons to the respective teams i.e., one colour to each team.

When the game begins all the players are ready with their ribbons.

When the facilitator says start, the players have to start tying one end of the ribbons to their feet and the other end to their teammate's feet next in line.

A time limit of two minutes should be set for the action.

When the game ends, all players stop the action.

Finally the facilitator counts the players in each team who are tied up with the ribbons.

The winning team has the maximum ribbons tied up.

17 COUNT YOUR STEPS

In this game the players need to hop, jump or run from one point to another in the least number of steps.

The facilitator should count the steps taken by individual players during the game.

There should be some time limit to reach the finish point.

Players who successfully complete the distance in minimum steps are the winners.

FOOTSTEPS IN A MINUTE

This game is a perfect warm up exercise.

Each player has to take as many steps as possible in the playing area in a time frame of one minute.

The rule is that every player has to lift his foot to take a step. The players can use as much space of the playing area.

The facilitator has to count and record the number of steps taken by individual players.

In the end, the player who managed to take maximum steps within the defined time of one minute should be declared as the winner.

19 BREAK THE WALL

Players learn to think logically and become active.

There is a lot of pushing, running, jumping and falling involved in this game.

It can be enjoyed more with a large number of players.

The facilitator has to help in forming two teams. The players from the first team have to stand in a circle, facing outside, hands tightly held, as if forming a strong protective wall.

When the game starts, players of first team, forming the protective wall are supposed to prevent the other team members from entering inside the circle.

The rule is that players from the second team are not allowed to use their hands for entering into the circle. The facilitator has to check whether players are following the rule. In the next round the task of the teams are interchanged.

The winner can be judged by the facilitator depending upon the number of players that are able to cross the wall within a time frame of 2 minutes.

20 HUNT 5 THINGS IN A MINUTE

Before starting the game the facilitator has to make categories for various household items. Categorisation may be as follows: wooden items, items made of glass, printed items, electronic items, items that run on battery, green coloured items, brown coloured items, etc.

To start the game, the facilitator calls out the name of any one category and all the players are supposed to hunt 5 things of that category.

Players who are able to hunt five things of the required category in the least time frame win the game.

21 Cross the River

This game involves physical activity with lot of alertness. It can be enjoyed with teams of large number of children.

Make an imaginary river in the play area.

Two distinct end points have to be marked in order to separate the river from the rest of the playing area. The players in each team have to stand in a definite pattern so as to form a bridge on the river.

The facilitator has to provide similar balls to each team.

When the game starts, the ball from one bank has to be transferred to the other. This can be done when the first player passes the ball to the next one and so on, by standing at their position, using only their hands and not bending their back.

If the ball falls from the hands of any player, he would be considered out.

The facilitator would pick the ball and hand it over to the next player of that team.

The team that is able to transfer the ball across the river in the shortest time by loosing least number of players wins the game.

A HALT AND A GO

This game is good to improve the concentration power.

All the players need to stand in a circle.

As the game begins, they are supposed to move in the clockwise direction.

The facilitator has to stand in the centre to call out the names of various things and creatures that exist on earth. E.g., albatross, camel, paper, tree, tiger etc.

The facilitator should avoid words often confused as living as well as non-living.

If he calls out the names of the creatures that move, then the players have to continue to move. When the called out name is of a non-living thing, then the player has to halt.

If a player does a wrong action, he would be considered as out.

Those who are out leave the play area and the game continues.

Those players, who remain in the moving circle till the end, win the game.

23 NECTAR FOR BUTTERFLIES

This game involves lot of running around in the play area. It teaches the player to be alert and active.

This game has to be organized in a large group of children. Some of the players have to be assigned the role of flowers and the rest as butterflies.

As the facilitators indicates the beginning of the game, all the flowers stand at different locations in the play area.

All the butterflies run around in the same area as if they are in search of nectar.

All the butterflies are supposed to hold hands once with each flower.

If they miss any flower or visit a flower twice, then they would be considered as out.

The butterfly who is able to finish the task first would be the winner.

24 MEDLEY OF FLAVORS

This game can be played in large groups. Children get practice of quick responses and alertness.

The facilitator can decide the difficulty levels for the players. In each team players can be assigned names such as SALT, SUGAR and LEMON.

As the game begins in the play area, the facilitator randomly calls the names of three flavors.

Rather than directly naming the flavors, the facilitator can also call the names of different food items containing those flavors. E.g. If the food item is ice cream, then the flavor involved is sweet, and if it is pizza, then the flavor is salty.

Accordingly the players respond to their names by sitting in their own position in the play area.

Any wrong action will make the player out.

Those players who remain in the game after 2-3 rounds should be declared as the winners.

25 STATE OF MATTER

This game helps to improve the concentration and power of analysis among children. They quickly react to any play instruction in order to achieve their goal. This game involves lot of mind and body exercise.

The facilitator can divide a large group of children into small teams of 4-5 players each.

In the beginning, the facilitator speaks out the names of common items that the children are familiar with.

The players have to act as particles according to the state of matter. If the facilitator call out the name of a liquid item, the players have to hold hands loosely, if he calls the name of a solid item, then the players have to hold each other tightly and lastly if the facilitator calls for a gaseous item, then the players have to roam about freely in the open space.

Any players with a wrong or delayed action should be considered as out.

Players with perfect actions all through the game finally win.

Far and Near

This game is helpful to improve the concentration of the children as well as knowledge about the location of different places of the world.

It can be played with a very large group of children.

The facilitator has to provide name tags of (either very far or nearby) places to the players before the starting of the game.

All the players are supposed to stand in 2 concentric circles. The players in the outer circle need to face inwards and those in the inner circle should be facing outwards.

As the game begins the players move in their respective circles in the opposite direction.

When the facilitator says "halt", then players stand face to face opposite to each other(in pairs) . If the players standing face to face have the name tags of places near to each other then they hold each other's hands. If their name tags have places far away, then the players move apart.

The facilitator has to keep a close watch on all the mistakes committed by the players. A pair with any fault would be considered as out.

The facilitator regulates the game till the end.

The pair, who continues to play till the end, wins the game.

Play while sitting and relaxing

In this section, there are games that children can play and enjoy by sitting indoors, at home, classroom, hall or outdoors like gardens, public parks and courtyards. These games involve writing/drawing/coloring on paper/paper cutting and pasting and other more creative activities. These activities are useful for developing finer skills among children. Word games described in this section can also be enjoyed at home. Children can be easily organised in such activities.

01 Coordination of Eyes and Mouth

Players enjoy doing facial and mental exercise.

We all open and close our eyes and mouth at various occasions in a day.

The rule of the game is that both the eyes and mouth need to open and close together at the same time.

Another rule relates to the speed of the game i.e., opening and closing eyes 60 times in a minute.

Kids are very enthusiastic to achieve the target in time. The game helps them develop their speed and concentration power.

Rubber Bands in the Fingers

All the players should be seated in the play area.

The facilitator has to provide a bunch of small rubber bands to the players.

The game starts at the same time for all. A time frame of 30 seconds should be provided to each player to tie as many rubber bands in all the 10 fingers.

After the time is over, the facilitator has to count the rubber bands tied on the finger of each player.

Player with maximum rubber bands tied on the fingers wins the game.

Note: The facilitater has to make sure that after the game is over, he removes all the rubber bands from the fingers of the players as this may hinder the blood circulation if worn for longer period of time.

Rhyming Words

This game helps to improve the listening and concentration power.

It can be played best again with a large number of players.

The facilitator has to divide the big group of children into various teams.

Each team has to secretly decide four rhyming words.

When the time starts, each team has to loudly, quickly and repetitively recite their words till the facilitator stops the timer.

The time given for one round should be 30 seconds.

After the time is over, each team has to guess all the words of the other team.

The team who is first in answering the correct words of any one team gets a point.

The team that is able to obtain maximum points after a number of rounds wins the game.

04 The Trio of Words

This game improves vocabulary and the concentration power.

One of the players starts the game by calling out any three alphabets.

The player sitting next in the group is supposed to speak three words with the respective alphabets called out by the previous player.

After saying the three words, the same player has to call out any three alphabets for the next player in the group.

As a rule, the words should not be repeated.

The game proceeds fast with only five seconds assigned to each player.

Those who miss out on words or are unable to respond in five seconds are considered as out.

As the game continues the child left playing till the end is the winner.

SORT OUT THE PULSES

This game helps to improve the concentration power.

Pulses like chickpea, kidney beans, soybean, cowpea, peanuts, whole pulses whose grain size is big and easy to handle for the children can be made available in bowls by the facilitator. Some empty bowls would also be provided.

The playing area can be a clean floor or a table.

When the game starts the players should be provided with a mixture of pulses. The quantity and number of added pulses should be the same for all players.

Each player is supposed to sort the pulses and collect in different bowls.

A sorting time of two minutes should be provided to the players for a mixture of five pulses.

Players who successfully sort out the mixture first win the game.

06 DON'T REPEAT THE COLOURS

This game helps improving the concentration power and memory.

The facilitator needs to prepare a number of drawing sheets with two similar sketches on them. As the game starts each player has to be provided with a single sheet along with crayons or oil pastel colours.

As a rule of the game, the players are supposed to fill different colours in the two similar sketches provided to them.

The time frame can be set up by the facilitator according to the age of the players.

Children with perfect colouring should be rewarded accordingly at the end of the session.

HOW HIGH CAN YOU REACH?

Youngsters enjoy playing with cushions and pillows.

This game will promote the ability to take risk to achieve higher goals.

They need to put the cushions one over the other and climb on to the top.

Kids gather a sense of achievement as they climb higher and higher.

They normally fall due to imbalance, but when provided with three chances in each round, they try hard and achieve their best.

WHAT'S IN THE TOFFEE?

Children enjoy playing in groups.

In this game there is a need to call action oriented sentences to the kids.

The facilitator needs to remove the verb or the action word from a sentence. Instead they need to call out the word TOFFEE.

The young learners guess the correct verb and remove the TOFFEE.

They can also play the game on one to one basis.

The children are elated when they guess the right word.

09 What's the Odd Word?

This game improves the vocabulary and concentration.

The facilitator has to make the players sit comfortably in a circle facing inside.

At random any player can start the game by reciting a set of words or a sentence with an odd word in between.

The player sitting next on the right side in the circle gets a chance to catch the odd word. If he is unable to do so, then he should be considered as out and the next in circle would get the chance.

The player with a right answer gets a point and the game continues.

The time given for each answer should be five seconds.

As the game proceeds, a number of players are out with every round. Only the winner is left playing till the end.

FIVE FOLDS – ONE PALM

This game improves the concentration power and the alertness of the players.

Before the game begins the facilitator has to be ready with a number of A-4 size sheets.

Each player has to be provided with a pencil and one A-4 size sheet. Players should be seated while playing.

When the timer starts, each player is supposed to fold their sheet five times using only one palm and write A-Z (26 alphabets) anywhere on the sheet.

The time period given for the task is two minutes.

Only those players who successfully complete the task in two minutes are eligible for the next round. The same act has to be repeated except that the time frame is reduced to one minute and thirty seconds.

The facilitator can reduce the time period with successive rounds that follow.

The player who continues to play till the end wins the game.

11 SEQUENCE UNLIMITED

The game is a test of language and memory.

The facilitator has to help the players to sit in a circle facing to the inside.

Any one player can start the game by speaking a simple sentence.

The player sitting next on the right side says another sentence starting from the last word of the previous sentence. E.g.,

1st player	—	I'll reach Delhi by train.
2nd player	—	Train is a fast means of transportation.
3rd player	—	Transportation means carrying people or things from one place to another.
4th player	—	Another good thing about Sohan is his good voice.
5th players	—	Voice quality depends upon many factors.

And so on.

Each player should be provided 10 sec to be ready with a new sentence. Those who miss the target time should be considered out of the game.

The winner is able to play till the end.

12 COUNT THE LETTERS

This game will improve the vocabulary, concentration and the thinking speed of children.

The facilitator needs to provide a writing sheet and a pencil to each player.

The players have to be seated in a circle facing inside.

Any player can start the game by calling a number E.g. if the number called is 7 then the player sitting on his right side has to speak a word with 7 letters, e.g., LETTERS. The third player calls out another number e.g. 8.

The next one in the circle has to speak a word with 8 letters. E.g., FACILITY.

Each player can be provided with a paper and a pencil to write words so that as soon as their turn arrives, they are almost ready with the answer.

In each turn the player should be provided only 10 sec to speak a word. The facilitator needs to check the time, the correctness of the word and the number of letters.

Players who are unable to speak the word in time should be considered as out. As the game proceeds, only the winners are left playing till the end.

13 Reverse Gear

This game improves the vocabulary and concentration power.

To start the game, the facilitator recites full sentences, phrases or single words for the players.

Just like the reverse gear of a vehicle, the players turn by turn speak just the reverse of the same sentences, phrases or word.

The facilitator also has to keep a check on the correct answers.

Players who have the maximum correct answers win the game.

HELLO!!

In this game players learn and practice better ways of communication.

The players need to be seated in a circle or in juxtaposition.

Children are fond of whispering in each others' ears. This game gives them an opportunity to do the same.

The facilitator starts by whispering 4 words in the ears of the first player. The words have to be in the following order: 1. Name of a place, 2. Name of an animal, 3. Name of a fruit/vegetable, 4. Name of a thing.

The first player, in turn whispers to the second one sitting next in the circle. By the end of the first round, the last player sitting with the facilitator speaks his 4 words loudly.

If all words are correct, the game proceeds. In case of wrong words or the order of words, the player who committed the mistake has to be traced.

To do this, all the players speak their set of 4 words loudly in reverse position in the circle (from last to first speaker).

As soon as the mistake is caught, that particular player has to leave the game.

In the next round a new set of 4 words is used. The game proceeds for a number of such rounds and only the winner is left playing till the end.

15 BALANCING THE HEAT

This game helps the players to develop their sensory skills.

The following items will be required for the game: a set of containers like glass, mugs, bowls, water in separate containers as hot, cold and normal and a thermometer.

The facilitator provides warm and cold water and target water (with certain warmth) to the players in separate containers.

Each player has to prepare water with temperature same as the target water, in their own bowls. They can check the temperature themselves only by the sense of touch.

The facilitator checks the final temperature of target water from the individual bowls of each player. He can do so by touching or with the help of a thermometer.

He also judges the time taken by each player to finish their task.

The player, who succeeds in balancing temperature of their target water with the given original water in the shortest time period, wins the game.

Card Hunt

This game helps to develop memory skills.

The facilitator has to prepare lots of white cards (3 inch x 3 inch) made from ivory sheets.

Before the game starts each player has to be given 10 cards and a pencil. The facilitator has to direct each player to write a name on one side of their card.

The players can choose the names from any of the following groups: Animals, fruits, vegetables, colours, cities, countries, sports, names of famous personalities, brand names, car models, etc. As the game starts all the players need to be seated in a closed circle facing inside.

One by one every player loudly calls out the word written in the card and places the card in an inverted position (word facing down) in the middle of the circle.

The facilitator can suddenly stop the players in between, randomly select any spoken word and choose any one player to pick the card carrying that word from the bundle.

If the chosen player succeeds to pick the right card, he remains in the circle, otherwise is considered out. With successive rounds, players leave the game and winner continues till the end.

17 Words to Express

This game gives an opportunity to the players to express themselves in words.

The facilitator starts by making a typical facial expression.

On seeing the expressions, turn by turn each player has to recite a sentence that fits in with that expression.

With consecutive rounds the facilitator has to show various facial expressions and the players need to speak out respective matching sentences.

For example: A worried expression – I don't know where I kept my purse, a jolly expression – Oh wow! I've scored the highest marks, a sad expression – Oh no! Today is our last holiday.

Players, who are able to promptly speak appropriate sentences in the shortest time, win the game.

Eruption of the Memory Box

This game enhances the memory skills and enriches the knowledge bank.

Before starting the game, the facilitator has to prepare a number of worksheets, each comprising of a topic written on top, such as the name of cities, companies and brands, TV programmes, coastal cities, historical buildings, sports personalities, celebrities etc.

As the game begins all the players should be provided a pencil alongwith the sheet carrying any one topic.

A time limit of half a minute should be provided to each player for writing as many names of the items from the given topic as possible.

The time limit can also be set by the facilitator depending upon the type of topics and the age of the players.

Players with the longest list written correctly win the game.

In the end the facilitator should read aloud the various correct names from the work sheets to increase the children's knowledge.

Train of Words

Children come across a large number of words in their day to day life. This game gives them the required practice to improve their vocabulary.

Before every round the facilitator has to distribute a paper sheet and a pencil to each player.

A time limit of 1 to 2 minutes has to be set for each round of the game according to the age and number of players.

When the facilitator gives the start signal, all the players are supposed to write as many words, one under the other in the form of a list.

The rule is that, there should be no repetition of words and the train of words should not include proper nouns.

At the end of each round the facilitator has to count and read aloud all the words in various sheets.

The player with maximum words in the train wins the game.

All in the Shape

This game improves memory, and stimulates the thinking and reasoning power.

The facilitator has to collect or prepare cutouts of different sets of things such as animals, alphabets, shapes of maps of various countries, continents, common household items like spoon, glass, jug, skirt, pant, comb, cricket bat, ball, badminton racket, lion, monkey, butterfly, snake, etc.

The front face of the cutout consists of the picture and the other face is blank.

When the children play, they need to be shown only the shapes of the cutout.

Only after viewing the shapes, the players are supposed to guess the correct item.

Children with maximum correct answers can be declared as the winner and rewarded accordingly.

21 Catch the Rhythm

This game helps to improve the listening and concentration power of the children.

This game has to be played with a large group of children.

The facilitator at random chooses 5 players to be the "hunters".

The rest of the players have to be seated in the circle.

In the absence of the hunters, the facilitator teaches a rhythm to the group of players. E.g., 2 claps-1 blank-1 clap- - - - -, 4 claps-1 blank-4 claps- - - - .

All the players in the circle start to play the rhythm continuously.

One hunter at a time enters the circle to identify the rhythm.

If he succeeds, he wins, otherwise the facilitator calls the next hunter.

Of the 5 hunters the one who is able to identify the rhythm in the shortest time frame wins the game.

The game continues with a new rhythm and a new set of "hunters".

WHAT'S MISSING? WHAT'S NEW?

This is a game to improve the memory.

The players are supposed to be seated in a circle facing inwards.

The facilitator has to provide different books to the players.

When the game starts, he introduces various books to the players in the circle.

Each player has a look at the book and passes it on to the next one sitting in the circle.

One by one, all the books are passed on to each player a number of times.

After the book rotation process is completed 3 to 4 times, the facilitator collects all the books and displays them in the centre of the circle.

The facilitator has to tactfully add or remove a few books from the original set.

The players are now supposed to view all the books kept in the centre and respond which ones are missing and which are new.

The player who gives the correct reply in the shortest time wins the game.

Words in Short Supply

This game is very helpful in building language and communication skills. It would also promote creativity among children.

This game can be played individually by the players or in teams.

The facilitator has to provide the players with a set of key words.

Using those limited number of key words, the players are supposed to create a meaningful sequence of events or a short story.

The facilitator has to judge the correct, meaningful sequence or story built by the players.

The team or the player who succeeds in shortest time should be declared as the winner.

Dancing Fingers

This game can be played when children are sitting in groups.. It makes the children more alert and active. It is also helpful in practicing spellings.

To begin the game all the players need to be comfortably seated with the facilitator.

As the facilitator puts across any English word to the children, they need to think and count the number of vowels appearing in that particular word.

The facilitator has to record the time taken by each player to answer correctly.

For each word as many vowels appear, that many fingers should be raised by the player.

Players who answer correctly in the least time win the game.

Foot Tapping

This game helps to improve the concentration and the listening power.

The players are supposed to be seated in a circle facing inside.

The facilitator moves outside the circle and stops near each player for foot tapping. The players close their eyes with the palm so that they can concentrate on the sound produced from foot tapping.

Each player is supposed to listen carefully and identify the number of foot taps made by the facilitator.

One foot tap denotes one word.

If the facilitator taps 5 times, then the player has to speak a sentence with 5 words. Each player has to be provided a time frame of 5 seconds.

The players, who are unable to reply in the time limit, lose a point.

The player with the maximum points wins the game.

Play Anytime and Anywhere

The third section of the book depicts set of activities and games that can be played at anytime of the day and in any kind of setting. The presence of parents, family and friends during the games at home and outside promotes development of a stronger bond with children. Children can also benefit from different types of play experiences at the same time. The following set of games can improve the whole spectrum of ability of the children.

01 Dancing Different Steps at the Same Position

This game involves simple dancing.

The first rule of the game says that the feet should fix at a position. If the players move to a new position, they are out of the game.

The second rule says that no dance action should be repeated.

The third rule says that all the players get the same duration of thirty seconds to dance.

Those who dance with maximum actions win the game.

The facilitator can play recorded dance music in the playing area. Music should be the same for all.

The facilitator has to count the number of actions of each player.

So, get set and dance!

02 Pouring Through the Funnel

Concentration is the key to this game. Even a slight distraction can spoil the rhythm.

Within a fixed duration of 60 seconds the children are allowed to pour full glass of water through the funnel to another glass and subsequently into other glasses one after the other.

Players need to prevent the water from falling while pouring through the funnel.

By the end of the desired period, the children who spill least water during the game finally win.

GUESS! WHAT'S IN THE JAR?

This game improves the child's sensory skills.

The players need to identify the contents in separate jars only through their sense of touch and sound.

Although a bit of preparation is needed for the game, the results are very encouraging. The contents in the jars can range from coins, pebbles, pulses, candies, gems, cookies, etc.

If transparent jars are used then the eyes of the players should be covered with a cloth or a paper strip.

The facilitator has to record the time taken by each player to identify the contents.

Those players, who correctly identify the items within the shortest duration, win the game.

Mirror Images

The very idea of aping others, gives a sweet tickle to children.

This game can be played with a large group of children and teams can be formed.

Herein kids have a great chance to build their concentration skills.

Players have to copy every action of their counterpart just like mirror images.

With one miss of action the player is considered as out. Those who copy perfectly till the end win the game.

05 WHAT AM I SHOWING?

It is a game of observation that can be played any time.

The facilitator needs to simply move any body part and the players are supposed to guess its name. This way children learn the names of various body parts.

The facilitator has to be quick in changing the movements in order to make the game more lively.

Balancing a Book on the Head

Be it physical balance or mental balance of the human body, it needs constant practice and training.

Regular acts of balancing help in developing control over the body and mind.

Balancing a book on the head is a simple game for the children.

They need to cover up a certain distance within a fixed time carrying a thick book on their head.

They need to prevent it from falling.

Players who carry on with the book for the maximum time period win the game.

Paper Tearing

Small children are best at paper tearing. When their favourite activity is turned into a joyous game then it gives them pleasure. The competitive feeling helps the children to work fast.

Players should be provided with waste papers of equal sizes.

The facilitator has to set the time limit of thirty seconds for all the players to tear their papers.

At the end of the defined time period, the torn pieces need to be counted by the facilitator in order to decide on the winner.

VISUAL MEMORY

It's a simple memory game.

Players can be asked to remember ten items kept on a table or at any corner of the room.

They can also memorise a few sketches drawn on a paper.

Kids use their brains immensely to finish their tasks.

The facilitator can provide three minutes for memory retention.

Each player has to be separately tested at different locations by the facilitator.

WHERE ARE WE?

Through this game children develop their memory skills and general knowledge.

The facilitator has to start the game by speaking one key word about any place. This word will act as a clue for the players. E.g:

Clue	Answer
Bells	– temple
Porter	– railway station
Check-in counter	– airport
Statue of liberty	– New York
Great wall	– China
Big mosque	– Jama masjid
Metro train	– Delhi
Char Minar	– Hyderabad

The player who answers first gets the point.

The player with maximum points wins the game.

Pick the Sound

This game develops children's concentration power.

The facilitator has to provide a writing sheet and a pencil to each player to note down the types of sound they hear.

When the game starts, the players have to listen very carefully to the surrounding sounds.

The time given to listen to the sounds is 1 minute.

At the end of that duration all players test the number of sounds they can recollect.

The player with the longest written list wins the game.

11 Blind on the Path

Children improve their imaginary and logical skills through this game.

Before the game starts, the facilitator has to demarket certain portions in the play area as the path. There has to be a well defined START and FINISH point on the path.

The player can view the path on the play area before the game starts.

The facilitator has to tie a cloth or a paper strip around the eyes of the players.

Each player with covered eyes has to follow the same path to cover that distance. If at any point the players put his/her feet out of the marked area, they are considered out of the game.

The facilitator has to record the total time taken by each player. The successful players who cover the same distance in minimum time win the game.

Photo Session

This is a game of creativity and imagination.

The players become models for a photo session.

The facilitator acts as a photographer with an imaginary camera. As he shoots, players have to pose with different poses and facial expressions within a defined time frame of 30 sec.

The facilitator has to continue clicking till the end. He also has to record the number of actions of each player.

The player who succeeds in creating maximum poses in 30 sec wins the game.

Knock-Knock

This game makes the children more alert and prompt.

It can be enjoyed more with a large group when played very fast.

All the players should be seated in a circle.

Anyone can start by saying "Knock-knock". Next player in the circle has to say "who's there?"

Third player says a name and a place that starts with the same alphabet. E.g. "Juhi from Jaipur", "Manu from Mumbai", etc. The time given to respond has to be 10 sec.

The players who miss out words or give a late response should be considered as out.

Those who succeed to play till the end win the game.

14 Greet Me Differently

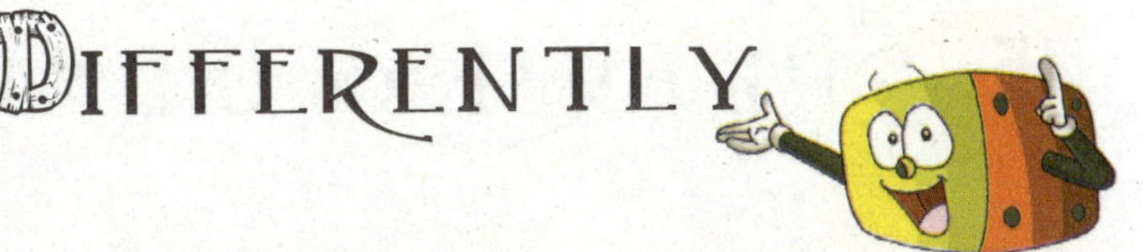

This game improves the concentration and alertness of children.

All the players need to be seated in a circle.

There are different types of salutations and greetings that children often use such as: Hi! (verbal), Hello! (hands shake), Hello! (verbal), Namaste (hands folded), Salute (right hand on the forehead), Good morning, Good afternoon, Good night, Happy Birthday, Sayonara, etc.

Each player has to speak a salutation or a greeting in their turn.

The rule is that, two consecutive players cannot repeat a salutation.

The game has to proceed fast. Any player with a delay or stopping should be considered out.

The player who is not out till the end wins the game.

15 Speaking Plants

This game helps the children in understanding the various parts and functions of plants.

It can be enjoyed the most when played in open gardens with trees, plants, and flowers all around.

Before starting the game, the facilitator has to make the players seated in a circle and assign different names of plant parts to each player e.g., stem, leaf, bud, flower, fruit and thorn.

The players speak words and phrases and even act like the plant part they are individually assigned. E.g. words like sweet smell, colorful and attractive for **flowers**; needle like, hurt, protective and hard for **thorn**, green, food factory and chlorophyll for leaf, etc.

As the game starts all the players speak turn by turn. Any player who says a mismatched word should be considered out.

The player who is able to respond correctly till the end is the winner.

16 THE GREAT BARRIER

This game is most suitable when played with a large group of children.

Two teams are to be formed conveniently with the help of the facilitator.

When the game starts, a member of one team does some action and the rest of the team members form a barrier blocking the view.

The players of the other team are supposed to guess the action from whatever little and scarce they manage to see from the other side.

The facilitator checks the action of the first team as well as the answer guessed by the second team. The round is repeated till both teams play equal number of turns.

When a team gives a correct answer, it gets a point. Facilitator has to record the points. The team with more points wins the game.

Foot Prints

This is a game of concentration building and body balancing.

Before the game starts, the facilitator has to make foot marks on the play area.

Turn by turn the players have to cross a required distance by stepping only on the marked foot prints on the ground.

As each player crosses the required distance, the facilitator has to record the time taken.

The players would be considered out if they miss any foot marks.

The player who successfully completes the distance in the shortest duration will be the winner.

18 JUNGLE VIBES

Children love to make sounds of various animals of the jungle and those seen in the surroundings.

In the play area each player has to make sounds of any one animal. e.g., barking like a dog, mewing like a cat, crowing like cocks, bleating like lambs, roaring like lions, croaking like frogs, coo cooing like a dove, mooing like a cow, hissing like a snake, etc.

The facilitator has to choose one player as a hunter. Eyes of the hunter have to be covered with a piece of cloth.

There can be large number of animal sounds in the playing area.

The hunter wanders listening to various types of animal sounds.

He has to catch one animal and tell its name. If the answer is correct then the player caught first has to be the next hunter.

The game goes on till each player gets a chance of becoming a hunter.

19 FIT IN THE NUMBER LINE

This game helps the children to learn to concentrate and act quickly.

Before the game starts the facilitator has to prepare hundred cards of 3 inch x 3 inch each carrying numbers from 1-100.

The facilitator should distribute one card to each player. One number-One card.

When all the players have a card the game can start.

All the players are supposed to stand in a line in the ascending order of numbers, one after the other.

The time given has to be 30 sec. Players who are unable to fit in, during the required time are considered out. Those who fit at the wrong position are also out of the game.

After the first round, the facilitator collects and mixes up the previous cards and redistributes for the second round.

Successful players continue playing till the end.

20 Throw, Spell and Catch

This game helps children learn correct spellings and improve the concentration power.

The facilitator has to make all the players sit in a circle facing inwards. He should also provide a ball for the game. As the game begins the facilitator recites any English word.

Any player can start the game by speaking the first letter of the spelling and randomly throw the ball to another player.

The player, who catches the ball, has to speak the second letter of the spelling and again throw the ball to the third player. The third player continues in the same manner, reciting the next alphabet of the spelling till the spelling is complete and the facilitator calls a new word.

Any player who recites a wrong alphabet of the spelling is considered out of the game and the next player continues with the spelling.

The winner is left playing and reciting spellings till the end.

WHO'S DOING IT?

Young children always look upon their elders for actions they enjoy and words they love to hear.

To begin with the game, the facilitator has to pretend to do certain actions or speak out the action words.

The players are supposed to pair those actions with appropriate nouns. E.g., the given action is run, the matching noun can be dog, for an action of crying, the appropriate noun can be a baby.

Children can play individually or in groups.

For every correct pairing, a point can be given by the facilitator.

Players or teams with maximum points win the game.

22 THE COPY CAT

This game helps to improve the child's memory skills and promote them to indulge in lot of physical activity.

All the players have to stand in a circle facing inside.

The facilitator has to stand in the centre to do various actions by using his body parts.

The players need to imitate his actions in the same order as the facilitator does them. After completing a full set of all the actions, the players are supposed to repeat the set.

The facilitator continues to do a number of different actions one after the other.

The players have to catch up with every new action that adds to the sequence.

Any player who is caught doing a wrong action or doing action in the wrong order would be considered as out.

The facilitator can add on more actions to the sequence with successive rounds of the game.

The player who manages to imitate all the actions in correct order till the end wins the game.

23 Linking Words

This game helps to improve the vocabulary and increase the thinking speed of the children.

This game can be played anytime with a group of children. Facilitator can either form teams or let the children play individually.

When the game starts, the facilitator provides a word to the first player.

Within 20 seconds the player has to speak out as many words associated with the given word. If the first player is able to speak out 3 words, then he gets 3 points.

The facilitator, then moves to the next player with a new word. Similarly the facilitator records the points obtained by various players.

The team or the player, who is able to score maximum points, wins the game.

24 East - West - North - South

This game helps the players to practice the sense of direction and the location of various places of the world.

There has to be a fixed play area for this game.

When the game begins, the player's eyes have to be covered.

The facilitator has to give oral instructions about the spot where the player is standing. (E.g., You are standing in Delhi facing towards north).

The facilitator also has to provide names of two people along with the place where they are standing. (E.g., Mohan is standing in Madhya Pradesh and Sonam is standing in Assam.)

The player has to locate both the people within a defined time limit of 20 seconds.

Each player can obtain a point for every correct answer.

The player with maximum points wins the game.

25 CAN'T DO WITHOUT IT!

Children can enjoy this game at home or in the classroom. The facilitator can either make teams or help the children play individually.

The facilitator needs to have a good collection of names of living and non-living things.

As the game proceeds the players encounter certain names put across by the facilitator.

In the shortest time they are supposed to point out name of one thing without which the living creature can't survive or the non-living item would be worthless. E.g., a plant can't do without oxygen, a fish without fins, a bird without a beak and an elephant can't survive without a trunk.

With a correct answer provided in the shortest time, a team would gain a point.

A team or a player with maximum points would be the winner.

Riding on the Newspaper

Children enjoy going for rides. Their play ride can be well converted into an educational one if they are provided with a piece of newspaper.

Each player has to be provided with a piece of readable newspaper.

The facilitator has to choose a set of alphabets for the players. Starting with those given alphabets the children are supposed to search and mark words from the given text of the newspaper.

All the players should be asked to search same number of words.

The player who is able to finish their task successfully in the shortest time wins the game.

POPULAR SCIENCE

2215 S • ₹ 135/-
Available in Hindi also.

2214 S • ₹ 135/- (Colour)
Available in Hindi also.

Set Code: 4514 S

- Over 900 Illustrations
- Over 800 Pages
- 890 Articles
- Four Volumes

Set 4 Vols.: ₹ 780/-
Each Vol.: ₹ 195/-
Available in Hindi & English both

HC009 • Rs. 620/-

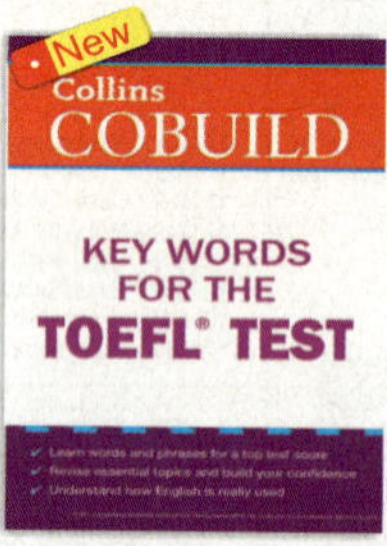

HC008 • Rs. 399/-

HC005 • Rs. 540/-

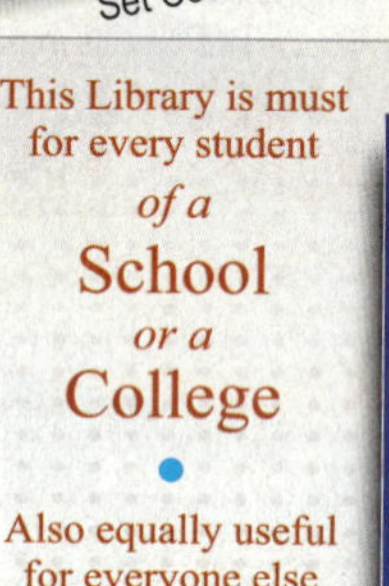

This Library is must for every student of a School or a College

Also equally useful for everyone else

Price: ₹ 600/-
Contains 4 books of ₹ 150/- each

9412 C • Rs. 120/-

6678 D • Rs. 150/-

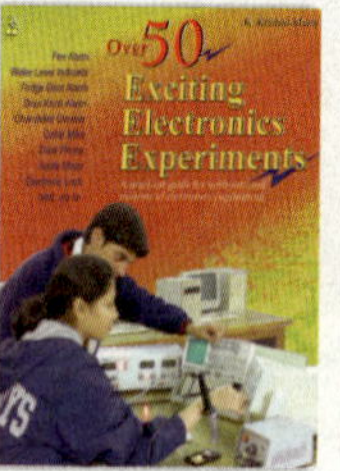

6679 A • Rs. 150/-

9660 K • Rs. 250/-

4 Books of the Library

₹ 150/- Page 256 (with CD) English Conversation
₹ 150/- Page 310 Grammar & Punctuation
₹ 150/- Page 316 How to use English
₹ 150/- Page 344 English Vocabulary

GENERAL BOOKS

9532 D • ₹ 250/- HB

8526 B • ₹ 125/-

9767 B • ₹ 150/-

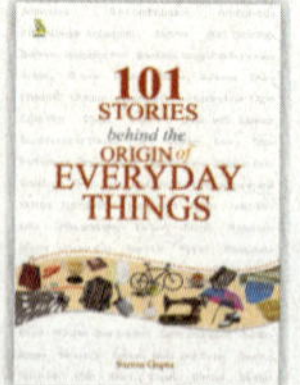

5114 B • Rs. 88/-

4175 A • Rs. 195/-

9821 K • Rs. 175/-

9459 H • Rs. 1000/- (HB)

9041 A • Rs. 195/-

4022 D • Rs. 100/-

QUIZ BOOKS

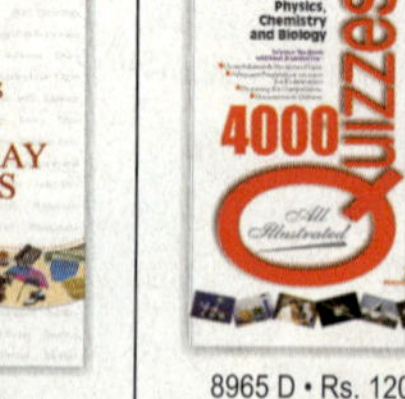

8965 D • Rs. 120/-

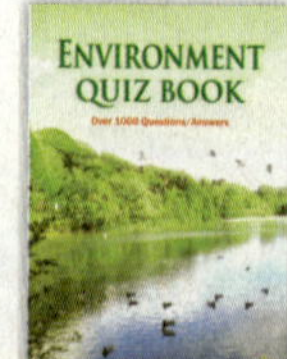

7726 K • Rs. 100/-

7727 L • Rs. 100/-

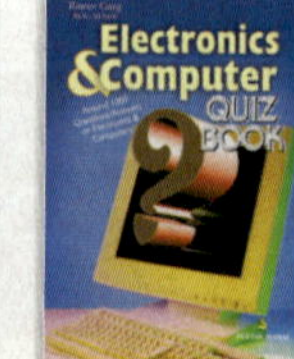

7723 F • Rs. 100/-

7722 E • Rs. 100/-

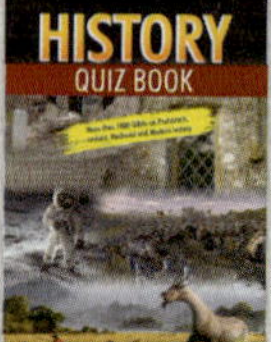

7753 G • Rs. 100/-

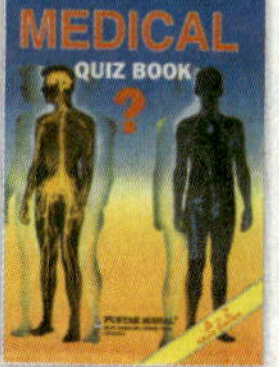

7725 B • Rs. 100/-

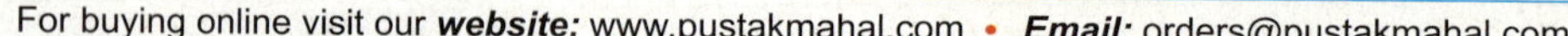

SELF-IMPROVEMENT

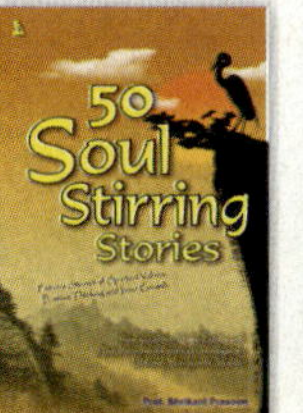

9491 J • Rs. 100/-

9498 C • Rs. 180/-

9490 H • Rs. 175/-

9464 R • Rs. 80/-

9096 B • Rs. 120/-

5614 E • Rs. 150/-

4008 J • Rs. 120/-

9026 D • Rs. 120/-

8885 D • Rs. 80/-

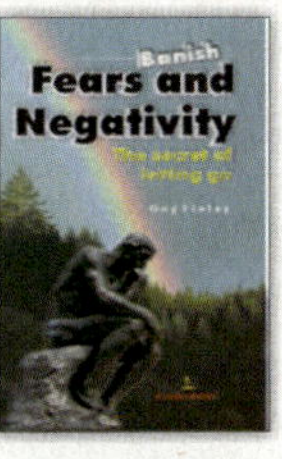

9027 D • Rs. 120/-

9081 D • Rs. 150/-

9091 B • Rs. 120/-

9060 B • Rs. 120/-

9969 A • Rs. 96/-

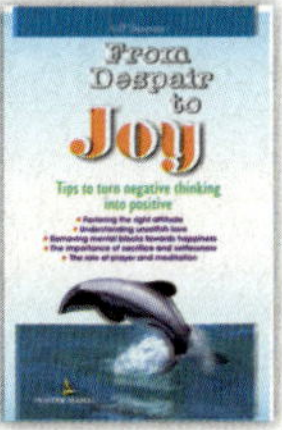

8928 D • Rs. 80/-

9449 A • Rs. 195/-

MANAGEMENT/JOB/CARRIER/BUSINESS & PROFESSION

All Time Bestsellers

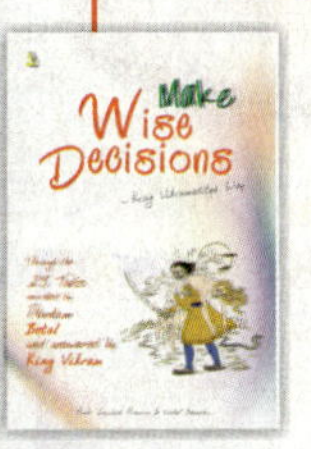

9461 K • Rs. 135/-

5338 A • Rs. 135/- with CD

8979 A • Rs. 96/-

9406 B • Rs. 150/-

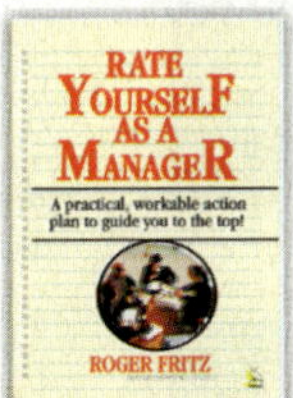

5441 D • Rs. 195/-

8883 D • Rs. 120/-

9672 G • Rs. 150/-

9682 D • Rs. 120/-

9404 D • Rs. 195/-

9313 D • Rs. 150/-

5623 B • Rs. 195/-

9439 L • Rs. 150/-

4017 D • Rs. 120/-

9431 C • Rs. 175/-

9402 B • Rs. 195/-

3403 C • Rs. 195/-

4004 D • Rs. 88/-

8990 C • Rs. 96/-

4018 D • Rs. 80/-

9079 B • Rs. 195/-

5618 D • Rs. 120/-

5640 C • Rs. 120/-

5615 D • Rs. 150/-

8972 C • Rs. 80/-

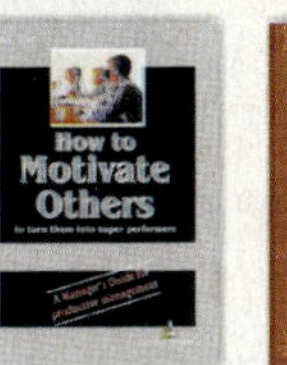

4001 A • Rs. 150/-

5646 A • Rs. 225/-

PERSONALITY DEVELOPMENT

9670 E • Rs. 240/-

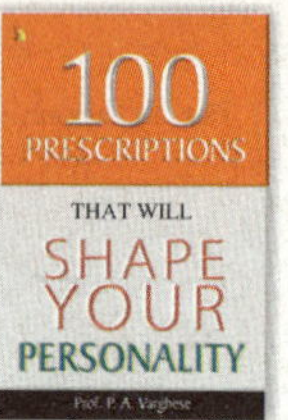

9678 R • Rs. 195/-

9450 B • Rs. 195/-

9487 E • Rs. 150/-

9466 T • Rs. 96/-

5639 B • Rs. 80/-

5641 A • Rs. 150/-

9088 C • Rs. 195/-

9667 B • Rs. 150/-

9666 A • Rs. 150/-

9696 M • Rs. 220/-

9973 B • Rs. 110/-

9981 B • Rs. 96/-

8868 D • Rs. 120/-

8966 E • Rs. 100/-

9070 B • Rs. 175/-

9028 D • Rs. 120/-

STUDENT DEVELOPMENT

9090 A • Rs. 195/-

97540 D • Rs. 175/-

9071 D • Rs. 140/-

9455 C • Rs. 150/-

5622 A • Rs. 108/-

9967 C • Rs. 120/-

2241 J • Rs. 100/-

9652 D • Rs. 120/-

8962 A • Rs. 100/-

9089 D • Rs. 135/-

4016 D • Rs. 140/-

4009 K • Rs. 110/-

8997 B • Rs. 120/-

4010 L • Rs. 100/-

SAYING/QUOTATIONS/PROVERBS

9474 F • Rs. 170/-

9953 A • Rs. 100/-

8947 E • Rs. 100/-

8999 D • Rs. 80/-

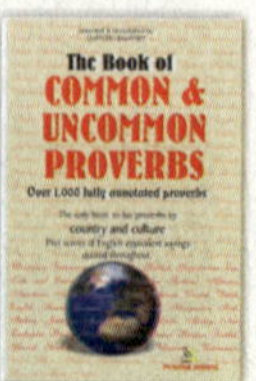

5512 A • Rs. 120/-

8963 B • Rs. 80/-

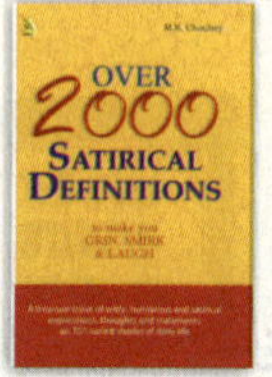

8890 D • Rs. 150/-

9925 A • Rs. 60/-

ALTERNATIVE THERAPIES

8882 F • Rs. 180/-

8879 C • Rs. 60/-

8983 E • Rs. 100/-

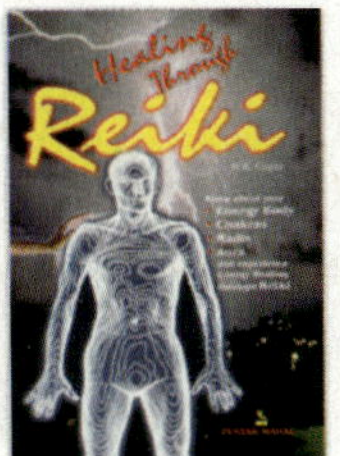

8842 D • Rs. 100/-

2317 E • Rs. 60/-

8889 D • Rs. 80/-

8836 D • Rs. 135/-

9935 F • Rs. 120/-

5637 D • Rs. 96/-

8281 A • Rs. 80/-

9950 B • Rs. 120/-

8941 A • Rs. 80/-

COMMON AILMENTS & DISEASES

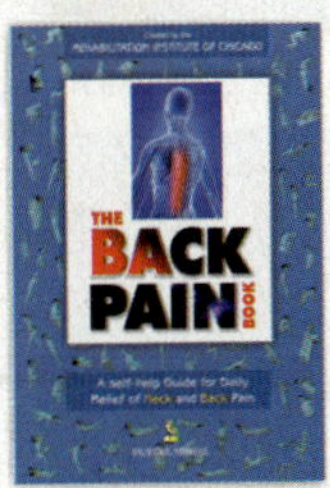

8891 D • Rs. 120/-

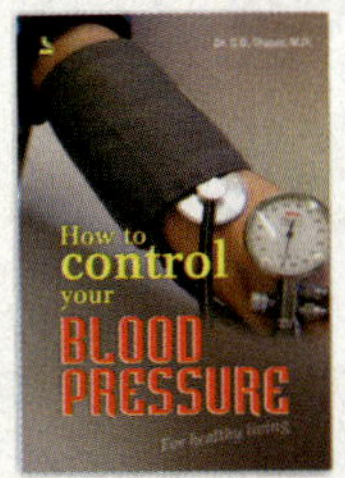

8094 D • Rs. 120/-

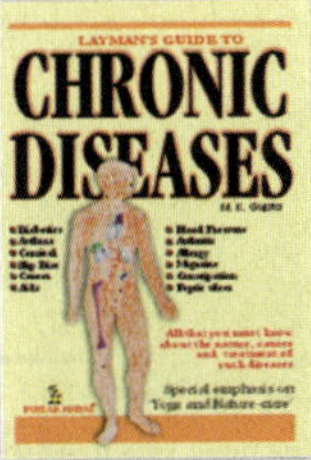

8848 D • Rs. 96/-

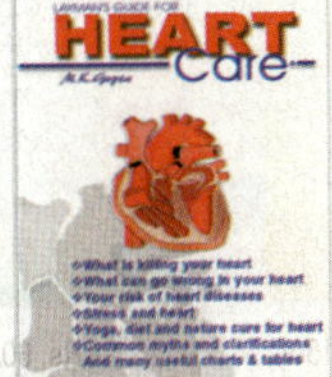

8888 D • Rs. 96/-

8908 D • Rs. 120/-

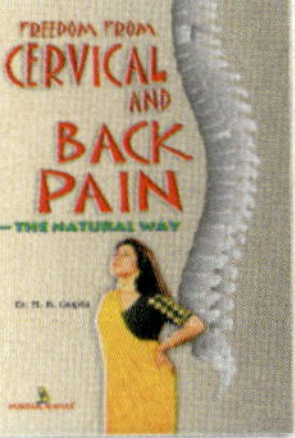

8878 B • Rs. 80/-

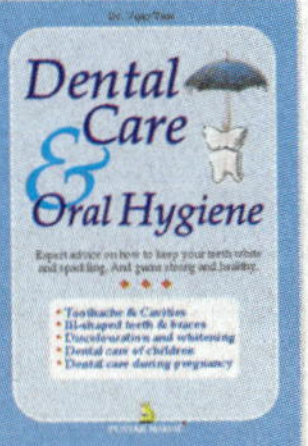

8964 C • Rs. 96/-

GENERAL HEALTH

9075 C • Rs. 225/-

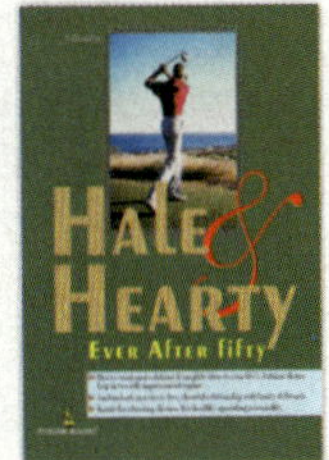

8939 D • Rs. 88/-

9039 D • Rs. 68/-

8859 G • Rs. 80/-

8877 A • Rs. 120/-

9940 D • Rs. 150/-

8948 A • Rs. 120/-

9038 A • Rs. 68/-

8847 M • Rs. 100/-

8870 D • Rs. 100/-

9025 D • Rs. 80/-

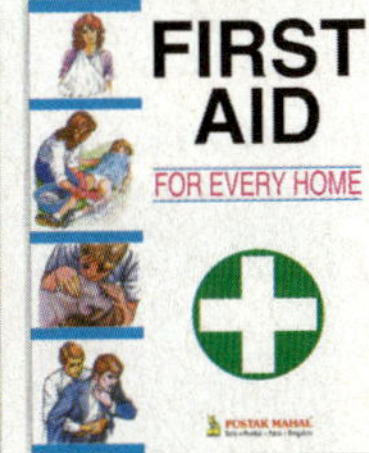

9902 F • Rs. 120/- Ⓗ

SLIMMING & FITNESS

8277 B • Rs. 120/-

8875 K • Rs. 120/-

9445 A • Rs. 150/-

HINDOOLOGY / RELIGION / SPIRITUAL BOOKS

9770 E • Rs. 150/-

9799 D • Rs. 160/-

9453 A • Rs. 195/-

4179 A • Rs. 295/- (HB)

4128 D • Rs. 295/- (HB) Rs. 250 (PB)

4181 C • Rs. 195/-

4177 B • Rs. 195/-

9997 C • Rs. 80/-

4182 D • Rs. 96/-

9984 E • Rs. 399/- (HB)

4130 B • Rs. 120/-

4183 A • Rs. 350/- (HB)

4151 A • Rs. 399/- (HB)

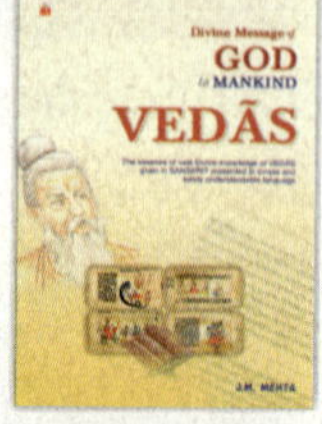

9811 P • Rs. 120/-

9585 A • Rs. 96/-

9405 A • Rs. 195/-

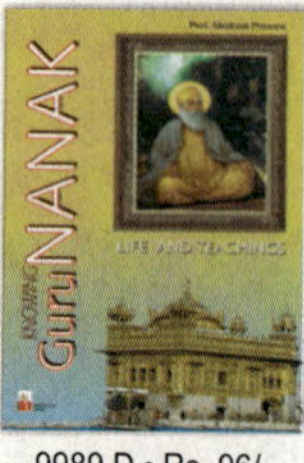

9989 D • Rs. 96/-

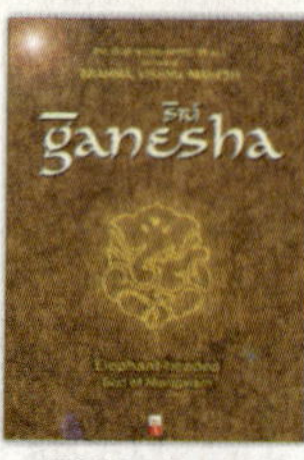

9508 D • Rs. 95/-

4134 B • Rs. 80/-

4188 A • Rs. 160/-

9504 D • Rs. 100/-

4133 A • Rs. 60/-

9513 A • Rs. 195/-

4126 B • Rs. 96/-

9812 R • Rs. 120/-

4152 B • Rs. 96/-

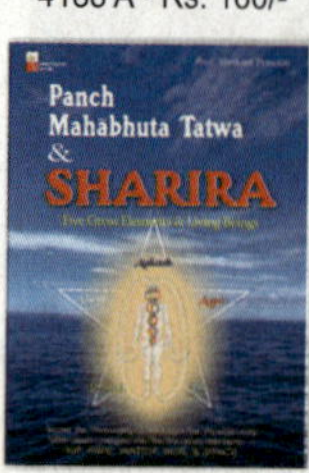

4407 C • Rs. 195/-

9504 D • Rs. 100/-

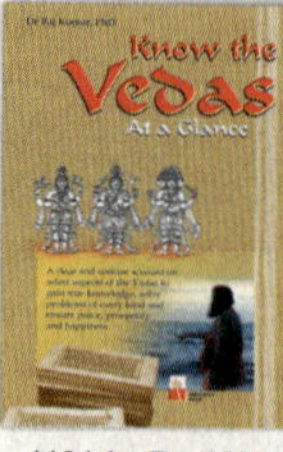

4124 A • Rs. 120/-

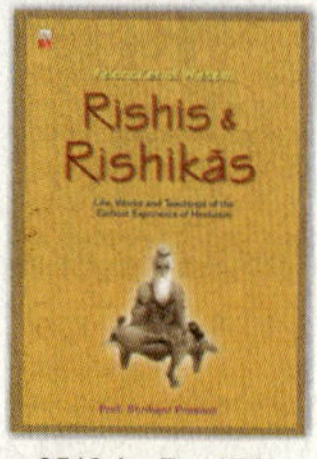

9513 A • Rs. 175/-

9520 D • Rs. 120/-

9987 E • Rs. 150/-

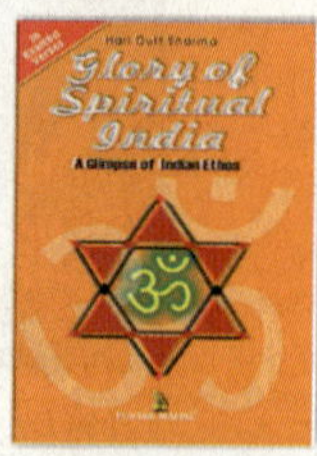

8898 D • Rs. 80/-

4190 C • Rs. 160/-

9509 A • Rs. 150/-

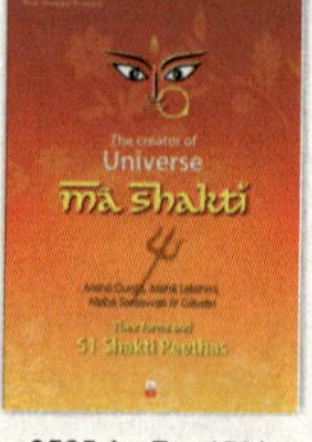

9525 A • Rs. 150/-

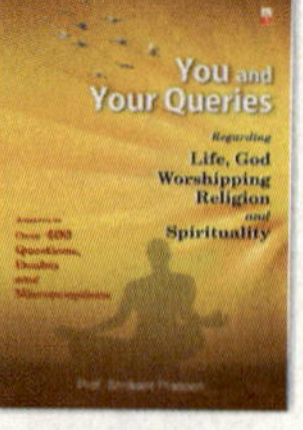

9540 D • Rs. 150/-

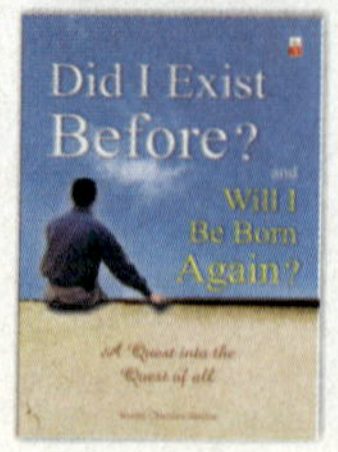

9542 B • Rs. 150/-

9514 B • Rs. 60/-

4132 D • Rs. 100/-

9069 A • Rs. 80/-

ASTROLOGY/VASTU/HYPNOTISM/PAMISTRY

9871 A D • Rs. 240/-

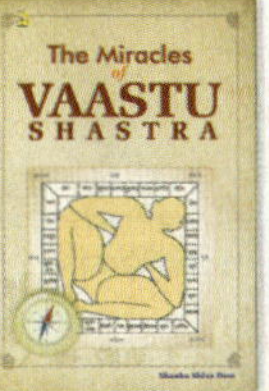

9693 H • Rs. 195/-

9671 F • Rs. 195/-

2127 D • Rs. 150/-

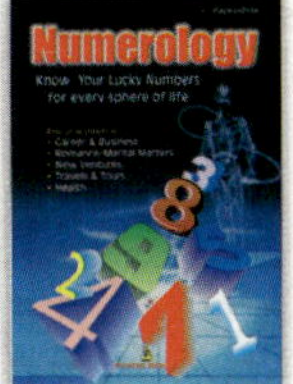

2109 F • Rs. 100/-

9086 A • Rs. 295/- HB

2116 D • Rs. 150/-

8259 D • Rs. 88/-

2109 F • Rs. 120/-

2112 D • Rs. 120/-

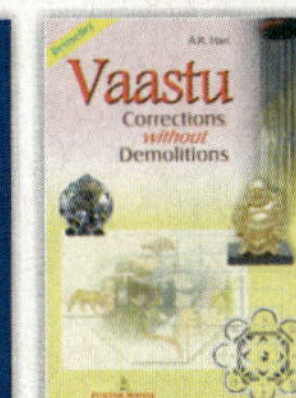

3110 B • Rs. 100/-

2133 B • Rs. 96/-

8899 D • Rs. 195/-

2125 D • Rs. 80/-

8925 D • Rs. 96/-

2132 A • Rs. 150/-

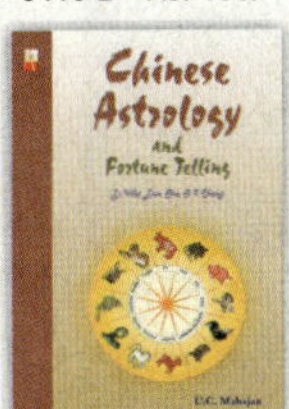

9432 D • Rs. 150/-

2120 D • Rs. 150/-

ENGLISH IMPROVEMENT

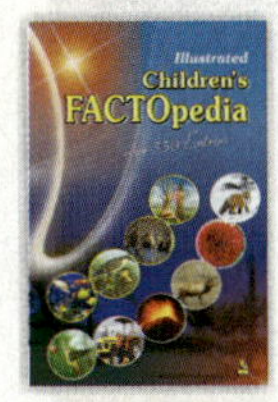

9496 A • Rs. 120/-

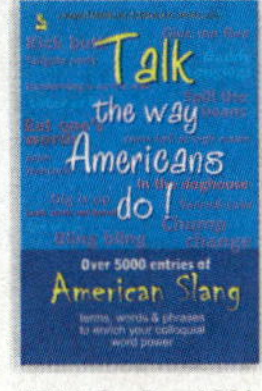

5541 C • Rs. 196/-

6651 E • Rs. 175/-

9448 D • Rs. 175/-

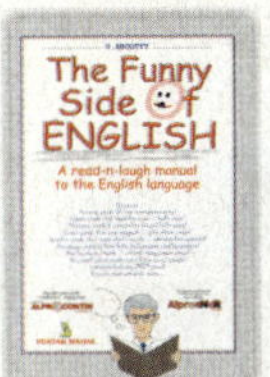

9056 A • Rs. 96/-

5538 D • Rs. 100/-

PERSON & PERSONALITIES

9669 D • Rs. 120/-

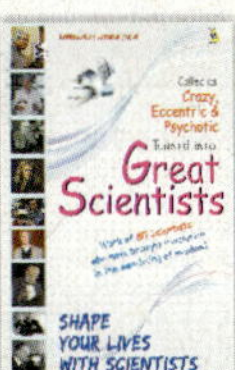

9825 E • Rs. 150/-

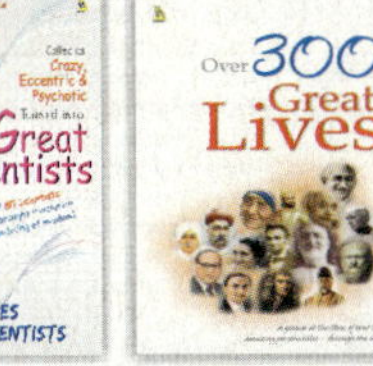

2113 D • Rs. 195/-

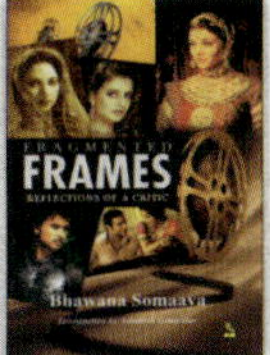

4170 B • Rs. 395/- (HB)

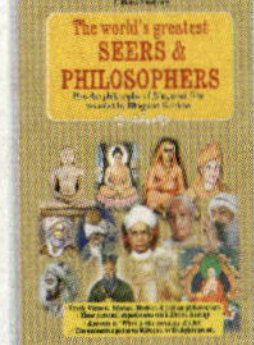
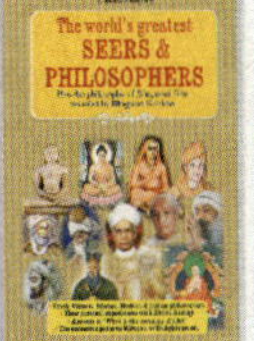

8991 D • Rs. 120/-

JOKES HUMOUR & SATIRE

2342 C • Rs. 100/- 2343 D • Rs. 100/-

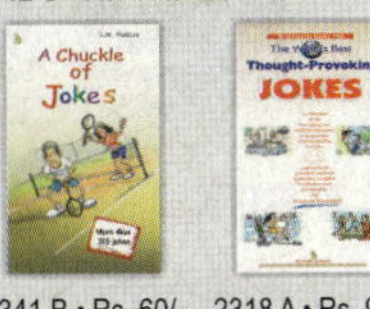

2341 B • Rs. 60/- 2318 A • Rs. 96/-

2330 B • Rs. 96/- 2319 B • Rs. 96/-

BODY/BEAUTY CARE

8093 D • Rs. 150/-

9986 B • Rs. 150/-

8971 B • Rs. 120/-

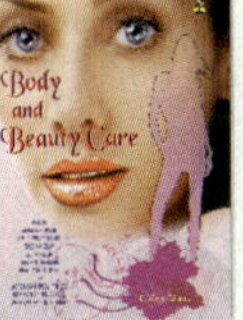

9922 F • Rs. 120/-

8865 F • Rs. 120/-

FICTION

FIVE BOOKS

Set Price ₹ 495/- ₹ 99/- Each Volume

Set Code SH 001

THREE BOOKS

Set Price ₹ 297/- ₹ 99/- Each Volume

Box Code 9795 A

THREE BOOKS

9752 B • ₹ 550/-

PARENTING

9906 J • Rs. 175/- (HB)

8261 D • Rs. 180/-

9674 J • Rs. 220/-

9784 J • Rs. 150/-

9594 K • Rs. 80/-

8917 D • Rs. 96/-

FUN, FACTS, MAGIC & MYSTERIES

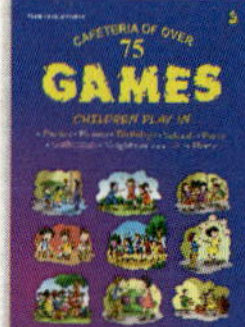

9484 B • Rs. 150/-

2275 D • Rs. 120/-

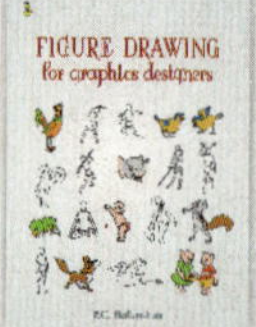

9479 M • Rs. 120/-

9470 B • Rs. 100/-

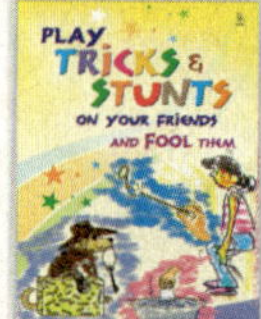

2208 M • Rs. 100/-

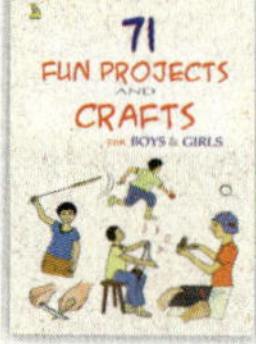

9816 D • Rs. 100/-

2247 F • Rs. 100/-

2250 A • Rs. 110/-

2211 F • Rs. 60/-

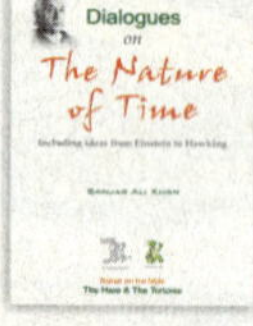

9457 E • Rs. 150/-

2237 M • Rs. 80/-

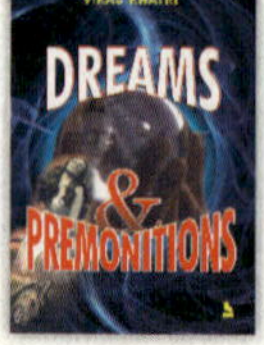

2335 A • Rs. 80/-

2243 L • Rs. 80/-

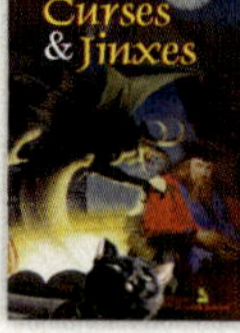

9985 A • Rs. 80/-

5110 A • Rs. 80/-

9040 D • Rs. 60/-

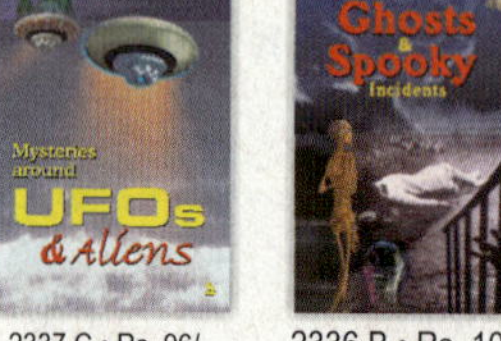

2337 C • Rs. 96/-

2336 B • Rs. 100/-

2331 C • Rs. 100/-

9977 B • Rs. 100/-

YOGA & MEDITATION

8269 A • Rs. 195/-

9998 D • Rs. 120/-

8939 D • Rs. 96/-

9080 C • Rs. 24/-

8867 D • Rs. 120/-

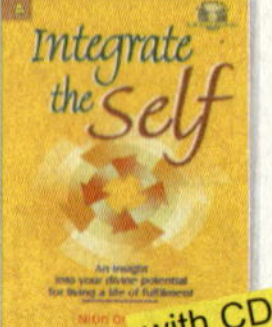

9958 S • Rs. 160/-

9087 B • Rs. 120/-

2118 F • Rs. 120/-

8901 D • Rs. 150/-

8099 D • Rs. 80/-

2119 G • Rs. 96/-

HOMEOPATHY, AYURDEDA

9446 B • Rs. 150/-

8887 D • Rs. 175/-

8270 B • Rs. 165/-

8010 D • Rs. 96/-

9094 E • Rs. 96/-

8944 D • Rs. 175/-

8923 D • Rs. 150/-

WORLD FAMOUS SERIES

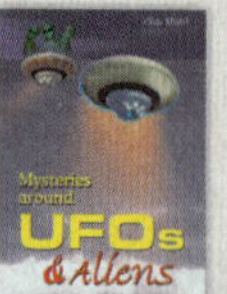

9472 D • ₹ 100/-

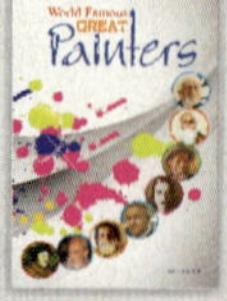

2337 C • ₹ 100/-

9483 A • Rs. 100/-

51107 • ₹ 100/-

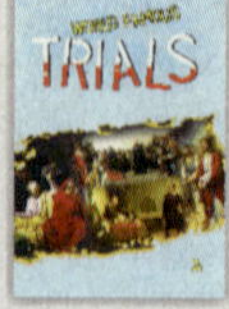

9766 A • Rs. 100/-

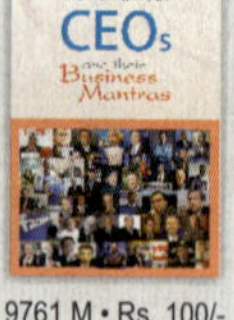

9489 G • Rs. 100/-

9761 M • Rs. 100/-

World Famous Mysterious Objects
True Stories of Mowglis and other Wild Childrens
World Famous Treasures (Lost and Found)
World Famous WARs & Battles
True Stories of Mystic Places
World Famous Adventures
World Famous Military Operations
World Famous Spy Scandals
World Famous Spies & Spymasters
World Famous Crooks & Con Men
True Stories 81 Weird Humans
True Stories of Great Explorers
World Famous Ghosts
World Famous Strange Mysteries
and many more.......

₹ 100/- each book

LOVE, ROMANCE & SEX

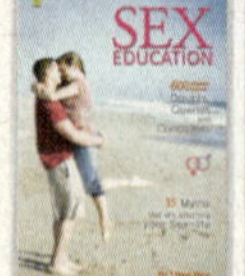

9602 B • Rs. 125/-

8260 D • Rs. 96/-

8266 D • Rs. 80/-

8278 C • Rs. 100/-

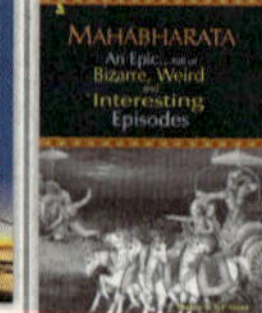

8916 D • Rs. 120/-

MORAL, WISDOM & FAIRY TALES

9677 P • Rs. 150/-

9486 D • Rs. 250/-

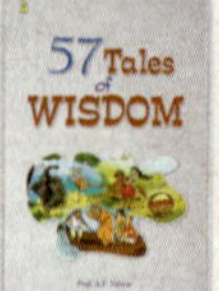

9763 P • Rs. 150/-

8967 F • Rs. 80/-

9077 E • Rs.120/-

9563 N • Rs. 125/-